GIUSEPPE
VERDI

Richard Tames

Franklin Watts
New York • London • Sydney • Toronto

Contents

© Franklin Watts 1991

Franklin Watts, Inc.
387 Park Avenue South
New York, N.Y. 10016

Phototypeset by: JB Type, Hove, East Sussex
Printed in: Belgium
Series Editor: Hazel Poole
Designed by: Nick Cannan

Library of Congress Cataloging-in-Publication Data

Tames, Richard.
        Giuseppe Verdi/Richard Tames.
            p.   cm.– (Lifetimes)
        Includes index.
        Summary: Examines Verdi's life and musical achievements in
        the context of his historical period.
        ISBN 0-531-14109-8
        1. Verdi, Giuseppe, 1813-1901– Juvenile literature. 2. Composers-
    Italy – Biography– Juvenile literature. [1. Verdi, Giuseppe,
    1813-1901. 2. Composers.] I. Title. II. Series: Tames, Richard.
    Lifetimes.
    ML3930.V4T35   1991
    782.1'092 – dc20
    [B]
    [92]   90-38303
                                                   CIP
                                                   AC MN

The Publishers have made every effort to trace and contact the copyright holders of the pictures on pages 5,11,13,16,18,23,27, but if anyone can give us any further information please could they let us know.

"Born in a poor village, I had no way to teach myself anything." When Verdi was old, rich and famous he liked to believe that he had risen from nothing. This was almost, but not quite, true. He was born into **obscurity** but not into poverty. And if he had no way of teaching himself, he did have a family and friends who soon saw that he had a talent which deserved teaching. Verdi's parents owned and ran the village "osteria," a sort of combined inn, grocery store and wine shop, near the market town of Busseto in Le Roncole.

Born on October 10, 1813, Giuseppe Fortunino Francesco Verdi gained his first introduction to music from the organist of the village church, Pietro Baistrocchi. He showed such promise that when he was eight years old, his father bought him an old **spinet**, which he was to treasure always. By the time he was nine he was able to deputize for the church organist. At 10, he was sent away to school in Busseto, walking home every Sunday and feast day to play the organ in the village church.

In Busseto, Giuseppe met Antonio Barezzi, the merchant who supplied the Verdi osteria with its wine. Barezzi, an avid amateur flute-player, was also the founder and leading member of the Busseto Philharmonic Society. Convinced of the boy's talent, he arranged for him to study with Ferdinando Provesi, the Philharmonic Society's musical director and town music master.

By the age of 15, Verdi was skilled enough to compose an overture for a local performance of Rossini's *The Barber of Seville*. At 16, he was deputizing as organist in Busseto,

Verdi's birthplace — a well-built but very ordinary country store in an obscure village.

Antonio Barezzi — "I owe him everything, everything, everything," Verdi declared.

as well as playing in Le Roncole, directing rehearsals and copying music for the Philharmonic Society, teaching younger pupils and playing the piano at musical evenings. He also claimed to have composed from his thirteenth to eighteenth year " ... marches for brass band by the hundred ... five or six concertos and sets of variations for the pianoforte ... many serenades, **cantatas** ... and various pieces of church music ..." (After he became famous, Verdi tried to prevent people from getting hold of these early works.)

When he was 17, Verdi moved into Barezzi's house and gave singing and piano lessons to his eldest daughter, Margherita. They fell in love.

Barezzi, now seeing Verdi as a future son-in-law, arranged for him to go to Milan to continue his musical education. A small grant was awarded to Verdi by a local charity but Barezzi himself was to pay almost all the cost of his lodgings and tuition.

In June 1832, Verdi applied for

Divided Italy

When Verdi was born in 1813, Italy was largely occupied by French troops. Indeed his own name was registered in the French style as "Joseph Fortunin François."

After Napoleon's defeat, the various governments of Italy were re-established much as they had been before his invasion. The south was ruled by a king based in Naples. In the center lay the Papal States, ruled by the Pope from Rome. Much of the north, including Parma, Verdi's home, was occupied by the Austrians. The rest was divided into small **principalities** and duchies. The only sizeable independent state was Piedmont, which was eventually to take the lead in uniting Italy under its rule.

At the time of Verdi's childhood, most of the people of Italy still thought of themselves as citizens of a particular region or city — Neapolitans, Romans, Florentines, Venetians or Genoese — rather than as Italians. Many were glad to see the French go and to return to the old ways. But some dreamed of freely elected governments or even a republic. In the north, where the French had been replaced by the Austrians, some dreamed of an Italy strong and united and free from occupation by the troops of any foreign power. Out of these dreams were to come the plots and uprisings and wars which together made up the movement for a reborn Italy — the Risorgimento.

Giuseppe Garibaldi (1807-82). With a thousand "Redshirt" volunteers he conquered Sicily and Naples to make a united Italy in 1860-61, but failed in his efforts to hold Rome as well.

The years of the galley slave

If it was Merelli who pushed Verdi to the brink of professional suicide, it was also Merelli who dragged him back. They met by chance on a Milan street one night and Merelli asked him for his advice about a new libretto, telling the story of the Jews in captivity in Babylon at the time of the famed king Nebuchadnezzar. Reluctantly Verdi took it home with him to read. Then chance played its part:

"I got home and with an almost violent gesture threw the manuscript on the table ... without knowing how, I gazed at the page that lay before me and read this line:

'Va, pensiero, sull' ali dorate'
(Fly, thought, on wings of gold)

The frontispiece of the piano version of *Nabucco*, the first of Verdi's works published by Ricòrdi.

I ran through the verses that followed and was much moved ..."

Three times that night, Verdi read the entire libretto right through. By the autumn of 1841 he was able to present Merelli with a complete score for *Nabuccodonosor* — later shortened to *Nabucco*. The première, on March 9, 1842, was a triumph. The audience demanded an immediate encore of 'Va, pensiero ... ' Verdi was suddenly famous. He was soon introduced to influential and artistic people who could help his career, such as the poet Andrea Maffei and his wife, Clarina, a famed society hostess. When Merelli commissioned another opera from Verdi, he told him to name a fee. Verdi went to Giuseppina Strepponi to ask her advice. Another success then followed in the form of *I Lombardi alla Prima Crociata (The Lombards on the First Crusade)*.

Feeling that he could now pick and choose, Verdi turned down Merelli's next offer and agreed to put on *I Lombardi* and a new opera, *Ernani*, at another opera house, La Fenice (The Phoenix), in Venice. The production of *I Lombardi* turned out to be, in Verdi's own words, " ... a great fiasco: one of the really classic fiascos." But he had better fortune with *Ernani*, a romance based on a highly successful play by the French writer, Victor Hugo.

Putting Venice behind him, Verdi then chose to adapt a play by the English poet, Byron *The Two Foscari*, for the Teatro Argentina in Rome. *I due Foscari* was well enough received but critics agreed that it was only good in parts. Returning to Merelli, La Scala and Milan, Verdi wrote *Giovanna D'arco (Joan of Arc)* in a few months. It was a modest success, but composer and impresario had a falling out when Verdi discovered that Merelli had tried to sell the score of the opera without his knowing, and then staged *I due Foscari* with the second and third acts in the wrong order. It was 25 years before Verdi agreed to write for La Scala again.

Verdi then moved on to Naples, where he worked with the local librettist, Cammarano, on *Alzira*, a story about a cruel Spanish governor of Peru. It was received with little interest in Naples, and in Rome it was met with almost complete silence. Verdi himself later said it was "proprio brutta — really ugly." As one critic pointed out, he was simply trying to produce too much — "No human talent is capable of producing two or three grand operas a year."

Despite this setback, Verdi immediately started on yet another work — *Attila, King of the Huns*. As so often occurred, the effort of composing gave him headaches, stomach pains and a sore throat. He completed the score "in bed, in an almost dying condition." Produced at La Fenice in March 1846, the patriotic theme of *Attila*, the defense of Italy against barbarians, aroused tremendous enthusiasm in the audience. According to Verdi's secretary, Muzio:

"the Signor Maestro had every imaginable honor: wreaths and a brass band with torches that accompanied him to his lodgings, amid cheering crowds."

But Verdi's illness worsened and his doctor ordered him to rest completely for six months, declaring that he could not "write music without grave risk to his health and perhaps even to his life."

By the autumn of 1846, Verdi was being pressured back to work by demands from music publishers and

Verdi in 1853 — well-dressed, self-confident and at a new peak of fame and success.

German Emperor Barbarossa in 1176. It was first performed in Rome in January 1849, two weeks before the city declared itself a republic when the Pope fled into **exile**. The audience loved it but it was too closely tied to the events of the day to prove of lasting interest. By the end of 1849, French troops had restored Rome to the Pope and the Austrians were back in control of Milan and Venice.

Leaving Paris, Verdi returned to Busseto to finish his next opera, *Luisa Miller*, another romance based on a play by Schiller. He did not miss fashionable society and was more than content to work quietly in familiar surroundings. Besides, he knew his own worth, as he once explained:

" ... I am more of a bear than before. I have been working constantly now for six years and wandering from country to country, and I have never said a word to a journalist, never begged a friend, never courted rich people to achieve success ... I shall always despise such methods. I write my operas as well as I can: for the rest I let things take their course ... "

Modern day productions of Verdi's operas show that his music lives on through another generation.

The tragic climax to *La Traviata*, Verdi's greatest success.

At times it had seemed that Verdi demanded more of himself than even his great talent could supply. Then came his greatest triumph — a succession of three masterpieces.

Rigoletto, based on another Victor Hugo play, is a story of cruelty, a curse and revenge. Verdi thought it: "the best subject as regards theatrical effect that I've ever set to music. It has powerful situations, variety, excitement, **pathos**."

The great Rossini confirmed the public's verdict:

"In this music I at last recognize Verdi's genius."

Next came *Il Trovatore (The Troubadour)* based on a play by the Spanish dramatist Antonio Garcia Gutierrez. The main character, the gypsy Azucena, is torn between a tender love for her adopted son and a driving passion to avenge her mother, who had been burned at the stake. The plot was very complicated and the music was very difficult to sing, but the theme was certainly as dramatic as *Rigoletto*. Most of the audience had not the remotest idea what was actually happening on stage, but few failed to be thrilled by the drama and excitement. At the opening night in Rome the audience demanded and got an encore of both the third act finale and the whole fourth act. The *Gazzetta Musicale* said simply that the music was "heavenly."

Verdi's triumph was crowned by *La Traviata (The Woman Who Went Wrong)*, based on the French writer Alexandre Dumas' sensational play *The Lady of the Camelias*, a love story that was both sad and scandalous. The first production was spoiled by a poor cast and hurried rehearsals but the second, in 1854, was a resounding success. It soon became the most popular opera in all of Europe.

Viva Verdi!

Opera played a particularly important part in helping to create support for the novel idea of an independent and united Italy. Whatever part of the country they came from, almost all Italians loved music and regarded composers, singers and musicians as popular heroes. In the Austrian-occupied north, public meetings were banned and the opera house was one of the few places where large numbers of Italians could gather together legally.

Verdi first hit the Italians' patriotic nerve with the chorus of the Hebrew slaves in *Nabucco*: "O, mia patria si bella e perduta!" (Oh, my country so lovely and lost!). *I Lombardi* struck a similar chord. When the Italian crusaders sang "La Santa Terra oggi nostra sara" (Today the Holy Land will be Ours), patriots in the audience cheered madly "Si!" The same effect was produced when the Roman general in Attila declared "Avrai tu l'universo, resti l'italia a me" (You take the world, so long as Italy stays with me.)

As more and more Italian patriots began to look to King Vittorio Emannuele of Piedmont as the future leader of a united Italy, Verdi's name took on a new significance. Shouting their approval of the composer, an excited audience could at the same time send a coded message of defiance — V.E.R.D.I.! — Vittorio Emannuele, Rei D'italia!

Patriots scrawl Verdi's name as a slogan of revolt while a look-out keeps a wary eye on patroling Austrian soldiers.

A National Hero

In 1853, Verdi and Giuseppina returned to Paris to work on *Les Vêpres siciliennes (The Sicilian Vespers)*, telling the story of a horrendous massacre of French troops by the Sicilians in 1282. Parisian taste demanded the spectacle of impressive scenery, lavish costumes, a massive chorus and no less than five acts and a ballet thrown in as well. Verdi commented: "A work for the Opera is enough to fell a bull! Five hours of music, Phew!"

He rose to the challenge, however, and the première, given in June 1855 during the Exposition Universelle, was followed by 50 more performances. The opera is now known as *I vespri siciliani*.

Shuttling between Paris, London, Venice and Busseto, Verdi found himself devoting as much time to putting on revivals or reworkings of his earlier operas, and making sure that nonofficial productions and editions of his music were stopped, as he did with new works too. *Simon Boccanegra*, the story of a pirate turned patriot, was a disaster when first produced in Venice in 1857. Verdi thought he "had done something fairly good, but now it seems I was mistaken." But a reviewer blamed the inability of the audience to recognize that the music was "very elaborate, written with the most exquisite craftsmanship and needs to be studied in all its details."

Throughout his career, Verdi repeatedly found himself having to do battle with political and religious **censors**. *Rigoletto* was originally

The official Ricòrdi edition of *Simon Boccanegra* — but even Verdi's official publisher cheated him.

Rossini (1792-1868) in old age. He wrote 40 operas in 20 years — then retired on the proceeds.

another new Verdi opera appeared — *Don Carlos*, based on another play by Schiller. It was premièred at the glittering Paris Universal Exhibition of 1867, but it was not popular and Verdi had to revise it many times before he was finally satisfied with it.

With 1867 came the death of his father and also that of Antonio Barezzi, Verdi's old patron. The composer played "Va, pensiero ... ," Barezzi's favorite piece, on the piano as he lay dying. Verdi well knew what a friend he had lost — "I owe him everything, everything, everything."

In 1868, the great Rossini, creator of modern Italian opera, also died. Verdi suggested that his memory should be honored by asking "the most distinguished Italian composers to compose a Requiem Mass to be performed on the anniversary of his death." It was a generous idea but received so little enthusiasm among his fellow composers that it simply fizzled out. But his own contribution, the *Libra me*, is recognized today as a great work.

1869 saw the opening of the Suez Canal and a brand new opera house in Cairo. Its very first production was a performance of *Rigoletto*. After many requests Verdi finally agreed to write a new opera especially for the new opera house. *Aida* was put together in just four months and for a fabulous fee. Set in "the time of the Pharaohs," it is a tragic love story staged on an epic scale. In Cairo and in Milan the audience enthusiastically agreed

with Verdi's own modest conclusion — that it was "by no means the worst thing I've written."

In 1873, the writer Alessandro Manzoni died in Milan. His romantic novel *I promessi sposi (The betrothed)* had been reprinted 118 times since it was first published. Verdi considered it to be "not only the greatest book of our age, but one of the greatest books ever to have come out of the human mind." As a tribute to the man he so much admired, Verdi proposed to the mayor and Council of Milan that he would compose and pay to publish a Requiem in honor of the writer if the city would pay for the first performance. Reworking some

Act II of *Aida*, staged at Paris in 1880. Verdi's huge reputation justified the expenses involved in such lavish productions.

of the material begun for the Rossini project, Verdi produced a score in time for the first anniversary of Manzoni's death. It was so much admired that three further public performances had to be given at La Scala, in Milan. After that Verdi took it on tour to Paris, Vienna and London.

In 1875, Verdi's special position as a national celebrity was officially recognized by the government when he was made a senator of the new Kingdom of Italy.

Verdi and Wagner

Verdi and Wagner were both born in the same year, 1813. Verdi became the most famous and successful composer of operas in all Italy. Wagner held a similar position in Germany. Naturally people compared their music. A number of critics thought that, over the years, Verdi's operas were becoming more and more like Wagner's. After seeing *Don Carlos*, the French composer Bizet declared "Verdi is no longer Italian; he wants to be like Wagner." Verdi was predictably irritated and retorted that "the point is not to know whether *Don Carlos* belongs to this or that system but whether the music is good or bad." Verdi did come to know Wagner's music; but he had little interest in Wagner's theories about how operas ought to be written and staged. Verdi's interest in music was intensely practical rather than theoretical.

He was, however, quite willing to adopt a new way of doing things if he thought it was an improvement. When he suggested to La Scala that the orchestra should perform in a pit so that they did not block the view between the audience and the action, he freely admitted "the idea is not mine but Wagner's and it is excellent." When Wagner died in Venice in 1883 Verdi wrote that "It is a great individual who has disappeared. A name that leaves the most powerful imprint on the history of art!"

Both composers were masters of "music drama," the art of blending the libretto and score so that words and music flowed naturally together to develop the action of the plot and the characters in it. But whereas Wagner gave more and more emphasis to the orchestra, Verdi always gave the human voice pride of place in his compositions.

Richard Wagner (1813-83). Verdi denied that he was imitating the German composer but openly admired his work.

A National Institution

If Verdi had his public triumphs he also had his personal problems. He had a falling out with the conductor Angelo Mariani and Giuseppina suspected that he was in love with Mariani's ex-fiancée, the singer Teresa Stolz. For years a shadow hung over their marriage, though there was never an open breach.

Verdi's old friends, the librettists Solera and Piave, died in 1878, and he found out that his publisher Ricordi had not been paying him all he was owed. By going back through more than 20 years of contracts, he obliged Ricordi to hand over 50,000 lire in unpaid **royalties**. The friendship between the two men was never really close

Teresa Stolz (above)**, costumed for the role of Aida at La Scala in 1872. Franceso Piave** (right) **— librettist for four of Verdi's best operas.**

again. Money also came between the composer and three different friends, to each of whom he had loaned money for theatrical projects which none of them could repay. And finally he had to sack his farm manager at Sant' Agata for losing the life savings of two of his servants in bad investments.

Most people imagined that Verdi's active career was now over, and that he would live out his last years in honorable retirement. In fact, his greatest triumphs were still to come. He was to owe them, at least in part, to another dramatic genius, Shakespeare. Thirty years earlier, Verdi had enjoyed a great success with *Macbeth*. For many years, he had worked on and off at an opera based on *King Lear*, but never felt able to do justice to the subject. Then, in 1879, the poet Arrigo Boito presented Verdi with a sketch for an opera based on the tragedy of *Othello*. Verdi expressed his interest in a rather offhand way: "Write the libretto. It will come in handy for yourself, for me or for someone else."

Verdi (right) **with Boito** (center) **and Ricòrdi** (left) **during** *Falstaff* **rehearsals at Milan in 1893.**

Otello — a great triumph but there was one more Shakespearean theme to be explored.

The project for a new Verdi opera after so many years was kept a close secret and the composer meanwhile worked on revising *Simon Boccanegra* and supervising a pet charitable project — a 12-bed hospital near Sant' Agata. It was not until November 1886, more than seven years after the idea had first been put to him, that Verdi was able to write "É finito!" (It's finished!). The première of *Otello* (the Italian for *Othello*) took place at La Scala on February 5, 1887. It was a sensation. At dawn the following day there were still crowds in the street shouting "Viva Verdi!"

Unmoved by applause, Verdi returned to the quiet life of a country gentlemen for almost another three years, much involved with his hospital venture. Italy was going through bad times and as a leading local figure Verdi also felt a strong duty to help his poorer neighbors by reducing their rents and creating new jobs by draining swampland and building new farms. Then in July 1889, Boito sent Verdi an outline for an opera based on Shakespeare's great comic character, *Falstaff*.

It was almost 50 years since the composer's one and only attempt at comedy, the disastrous *Un Giorno di Regno*. Yet he was immediately attracted to the idea. He was held back by the thought of "the enormous number of my years." He was, after all, nearly 77 years old. Boito's reply was to challenge the critics who had said that *Otello* was his final masterpiece.

Boito and Verdi at Sant' Agata. Their collaboration gave the composer his greatest successes.

Verdi agreed, but he was no longer "the galley slave," turning out one opera after another. He limited himself to two hours composing a day. Over a year later he was still grinding away at his task, though he found it no heavy labor: "I am enjoying myself writing the music. I have no plans for it and I don't even know if I shall finish it ... "

In fact it took the better part of three years to complete, and then Verdi attended the rehearsals although he was now in his 80th year.

The première of *Falstaff* at La Scala on February 9, 1893 was yet another triumph. At the opening night in Rome, the king summoned Verdi to the royal box where he was left alone to receive the thunderous congratulations of the audience.

Verdi's last project combined charity with music, planning the building of The Casa di Riposa per Musicisti, a rest home for 100 retired musicians who were too poor or too ill to live alone. The

Music made Verdi a rich man. He acknowledged his good fortune by funding this elegant rest home for musicians.

architect was Boito's brother and the composer worked as closely with him as he had with the librettist. In his will Verdi left the royalties of all his operas to complete and support what he called "my greatest work."

Verdi was still composing, but his last works were church music, *Four Sacred Pieces*, premièred in Paris during Holy Week in 1898. Giuseppina had died in 1897, leaving Verdi totally bereft by her absence. He all but abandoned Sant' Agata in favor of a suite in the Grand Hotel, Milan. He died there on January 27, 1901 of a stroke.

Verdi asked in his will not to have a great public funeral. He wanted a simple service, "very modest, either at dawn or at the time of the *Ave Maria* in the evening, without music and singing." He was buried beside Giuseppina but when the musicians' rest home was completed, their coffins were removed to be reburied there. At the gates of the cemetery the conductor Arturo Toscanini led a chorus of 800 singing "Va, pensiero ... " Princes and other important figures led the funeral procession while 200,000 onlookers lined the streets of Milan.

An Italian artist imagines Verdi summoning up the spirits of Otello and Desdemona.

Sant' Agata

Verdi bought his estate at Sant' Agata, near Busseto, in 1848 but did not really settle in until 1851 when Giuseppina Strepponi came with him. As they were not actually married until 1859, the townspeople of Busseto were scandalized. Giuseppina was musically gifted, kind and charitable and a wealthy and successful woman in her own right. If local gossips could not respect her for her own qualities, Verdi refused to have anything to do with them.

So they lived a rather secluded life — planting a fine garden around their home and taking an avid and detailed interest in the farms on their estate. The peace and quiet helped Verdi to compose but sometimes he went to Sant' Agata to get away from music entirely. For long periods he was content to live the life of a country gentleman — improving his land and buildings, walking and shooting in the woods, and passing the evenings at dinner and playing cards with old friends.

The villa at Sant' Agata where Verdi lived out a peaceful but productive retirement.

Find out More ...

Important Books

On Verdi
Anvil Chorus by Shane Stevens (Delacorte, 1985)
Verdi in the Age of Italian Romanticism by David R. Kimbell (Cambridge University Press, 1985)
Aspects of Verdi by George Martin (Dodd Mead, 1988)
Opera by John Nicholas (Oxford University Press, 1986)

On Italy
Garibaldi by Nina B. Baker (Vanguard, 1944)

Important Dates

1813 Born at Le Roncole, Parma
1823 Moves to Busseto.
1831 Rejected by Milan Conservatory
1836 Marries Margherita Barezzi
1838 Death of his son
1839 Première of *Oberto, Conte di San Bonifacio*; death of his daughter
1840 Death of his wife, Margherita
1842 Première of *Nabucco*
1847 *Macbeth*; visits London and Paris
1848 Buys estate at Sant' Agata
1851 *Rigoletto*
1853 *Il Trovatore* and *La Traviata*

1859 Marries Giuseppina Strepponi
1860 Elected to the Italian parliament
1862 Visits Russia; *La forza del destino*
1871 *Aida*
1874 *Requiem* for Manzoni
1875 Is made a senator
1887 *Otello*
1893 *Falstaff*
1896 Begins building musicians' rest home
1897 Death of Giuseppina
1898 *Four Sacred Pieces*
1901 Dies in Milan

Glossary

Cantata   A musical composition originally with one spoken voice and a solo instrument. Today it can also mean a choral work for concert performances.

Censors   Officials who would study books, plays, operas, etc., to judge their suitability for public viewing. They could ban publications or performances if something was felt unsuitable.

Duchy   The territory of a duke.

Exile   To go into exile is to be forced to leave the country.

Impresario   The manager of an opera company.

Libretto   The book of words (script) of an opera.

Obscurity   Unknown to fame.

Pathos   The ability that raises pity and sorrow.

Première   The first public performance of a play, opera, ballet, etc.

Principalities   The territory of a prince.

Royalties   Payments to authors, composers, etc., for every copy sold or public performance of their work.

Spinet   A musical instrument similar to a small harpsichord.

Index

Picture Acknowledgements

The publishers would like to thank the following for their kind permission to reproduce their photographs in this book: English National Opera 14,25; Julian Budden 16,18; La Scala Museum, Milan 6,7 (top); Mansell Collection 8,24; Mary Evans Picture Library frontispiece, 14,19,20,21,22,28,29,32; Robert Harding Picture Library 7 (bottom); Royal College of Music cover; Royal Opera House 9,15,17,26.